# WHAT IS A PUPPY?

Puppies are a wet nose, a squeal, a warm, soft belly and a wagging tail. They come in all shapes and sizes, fuzzy or close-coated, and run the gamut in color and markings. But, there is one thing that all puppies have in common—*appeal*, and this can be your undoing. Too many people are caught in the strands of this emotional web, trapped by a pair of bright eyes, a wiggling warmth and a tiny, licking pink tongue. Their normal business sense, as well as common sense, smothered by the wonder of this little ball of living love, they make their purchase without regard for their basic needs in their choice of a canine companion. And when they do, they have made their first drastic mistake.

When you consider purchasing any appliance for the home you normally do a good deal of shopping around to find the make and kind that fits your

**Bright eyes, fuzzy coat, and overall cuddliness make this puppy hard to resist.**

plan of living. When you are on the verge of buying a new car you consider a great variety of things: the terrain over which you must travel, the size you want, the horsepower, the conditions under which your car will be used, the color, your mode of living and the necessary performance you want from the machine. But, when you contemplate buying a puppy, you forget the sensible approach and generally buy blindly, even though this pup you buy will probably outlast the appliance or the car you've thought about so much.

The moral of this is, of course, use your mentality and common sense when buying a puppy. You will have to live with him a long time and it might just as well be a pleasant association. It will be, if you use your brains at the outset. Believe me, your heart will be involved soon enough.

**When you buy a puppy, you should know its background and growth potential. For example, this tiny Great Dane will grow to be a dog of enormous size, with an appetite to match!**

## SIZE CONSIDERATION

There is not a great deal of difference in the size of very young puppies. The Great Dane, St. Bernard or Irish Wolfhound puppy disguises its eventual mature size and, unless the buyer is aware of the huge size to which these animals can grow, an apartment dweller may later find himself in a small area completely surrounded by dog.

The larger breeds make wonderful pets and companions; but they need room, and the buyer of a tiny pup should know the complete background of his puppy, realize its growth potential and be prepared to have sufficient area for it when it reaches full maturity.

Puppies need care (as does the grown dog) and the larger the breed the greater the care generally. Grooming a large dog takes more time and effort than grooming a small dog, coats being equal. Sheer area to cover during the process of grooming makes this so.

Large dogs consume more food than small dogs and the owner must be more careful with their feeding. This is because it takes them longer to reach maturity, and when they do, they will exhibit a lack of nutritional elements more obviously than will a smaller dog. The larger breeds should also be more completely trained than is necessary for smaller breeds, for they must be under control at all times. Small dogs are easier to travel with than large dogs and may be accepted at hotels or motels that would not tolerate big breeds. They can also be spirited into a motel room, if necessary, without, you hope, being seen by the manager. It would be both unwise and ridiculous to attempt to sneak a Great Dane into a room under similar circumstances.

From the preceding it might seem that I advocate the smaller breeds of canines. This is not a fact. I am simply reporting objectively. The larger breeds of dogs are more of a chore to keep and feed, but are well worth the extra time and trouble involved. As a matter of record I have been associated with many breeds of dogs, and I prefer the larger breeds. By choice I have been most closely associated over the years with the German Shepherd Dog.

## COAT CONSIDERATION

The kind and quality of coat your puppy will assume when it reaches maturity is another consideration for the neophyte buyer. Long-coated breeds need more coat care than short-coated breeds, and some breeds need often expensive, expert clipping or plucking to keep them looking their best.

Remember that, depending on the seasons, the climate in which they live, and the hours they spend indoors and outdoors, dogs shed. Long hairs and fuzzy undercoat are more difficult to pick up with a vacuum or carpet sweeper, and light colored hair is much more obvious on dark upholstery and rugs than

Some breeds, such as the Old English Sheepdog, will grow profusely long coats upon maturity. Be prepared for extensive grooming and shedding should you purchase a heavily coated dog.

dark colored hair, and vice versa. This does not mean that I advocate buying a dog whose hair color matches your home decorative scheme. There are too many other factors that must be considered and that are more important.

design of usefulness you had projected for the dog you own. Study other breeds then, until you find the *right dog for you.*

If you are the nervous type, perhaps a breed that is quiet and lethargic would be best for you, a dog that can act as a counter-balance to

Shibas and Boxers are equally cute as puppies, but when they mature they are completely different dogs, each with its own breed-specific characteristics. Learn as much as you can about the different breeds and try to buy the type of dog that best complements your lifestyle and personality.

## CONSIDERATION OF BREED CHARACTERISTICS

Here we have the most important consideration of all. Breeds of dogs, like races of people, have certain characteristics. Before buying, select the breed which you think is most suited to you and study the basic breed characteristics. Perhaps, after study, you will find that the breed you considered purchasing had eye appeal (and suited your sense of beauty) but does not particularly fit into the pattern of your life or the

your own personality and bring you a measure of calmness. Or it may be that you are the kind of person who needs an energetic, extremely alert animal to bolster your own lack in this direction. Possibly, if you yourself are quiet and a seeker of peace, the aggressive, too quick animal might constitute a nuisance and an irritation to you. Then you need a dog who mirrors your own character.

If you pick the wrong breed, the one whose characteristics do not fit or embellish your own character pattern or way of life, the result could be a personality clash between dog and owner. There would be a complete lack of the companionship that should exist between you and your dog.

Another important consideration, which also has to do with breed characteristics, is the purpose the a fast, wide-ranging breed. Your selection for a future easy and pleasurable day of hunting should be from one of the slower gundog breeds, perhaps a German Shorthaired Pointer.

If you want a puppy to grow into a guard dog, the breed to select from is one that has been specifically bred for that purpose.

**Select the dog that has been specifically bred for the purpose you have in mind. The German Shorthaired Pointer, for instance, is an excellent gundog breed.**

adult dog will fulfill. If you like to hunt, what better choice could there be for you than a puppy of one of the gundog breeds, a hound, a bird dog, or a retriever, according to your hunting preference. Here too, one must consider the genetic heritage or characteristics of the various gundog breeds to meet your specific need. As an example let us assume that you are a field enthusiast but rather advanced in years, or you have some physical handicap, but still like to hunt. Common sense should tell you that you should not select a puppy of

Though there are exceptions to every rule, you are more apt to get the kind of dog you want if you pick a puppy of a breed that has been bred for generations and selected for the particular purpose you have in mind. Don't buy a puppy of a working breed and try to turn him into a gundog or vice versa. The breeds of dogs, through selective breeding, have been molded mentally and physically to certain utilitarian ends. To attempt to channel them to other purposes is generally futile and unrewarding.

One of the first decisions a puppy buyer must make is whether to buy a mongrel or a purebred puppy.

# PUREBRED OR MONGREL?

The question of whether to buy a mongrel, a crossbred or a purebred puppy can produce constant argument between dog novices. To the "true" dog person, there can be no question, only the purebred puppy is worthy of consideration. Undoubtedly mongrels and crossbreds make excellent pets and are loyal, intelligent and loving. They possess the unusual vigor which hybridizing so frequently engenders. As puppies they are cute and lovable. But remember all puppies are cute and lovable and not much different to the undiscerning eye. The tiny mongrel you buy and take home may grow into a nondescript, oversized monster with a Great Dane or a St. Bernard lurking unknown in his geneology. On the other hand you are certain that the purebred pup will reach a certain size and weight, sport a specific type of coat and generally look, act and react, upon maturity, in keeping with the specifications of his breed.

Though many mongrels make excellent watchdogs and companions, even hunters, they are not specialists in any particular field due to the mixture of their ancestry. And, there are any number of purebred dogs that would generally surpass the mongrel at any job if they are bred for that specific purpose.

Crossbreds are generally animals crossed for a purpose. Setter and Pointer crosses produce shorthaired dogs that are excellent in the field. But, again, they are not more excellent than purebred specimens of either of the crossed breeds. Several of the species of coonhounds are frequently crossed and, in the

Crossbreeds can make loyal, loving pets. However, you will have no idea what your mongrel puppy will grow up to become. Size, personality, disposition, and other traits are all up to pot luck.

A crossbreed such as this Lhasa Apso-Cocker Spaniel mix is generally an intentional breeding for a specific purpose.

crossing, produce typical hounds that are good trailing dogs. In the north, sled dog breeds are crossed and often the dogs used for this work are actually mongrels. Again it is questionable whether these crossbreds and mongrels are as dependable and fit as the purebreds, selected and bred through generations for their specific task.

A mongrel is a dog bred from undistinguished parents who carry, in their germ plasm, the characteristics of many breeds. They are the result of a mistake, for no one breeds mongrels deliberately. The great variety of genetic combinations that occur from such a mating makes it impossible to determine what the mongrel will look like upon maturity. Many novices think that if they see the mother of the pups they can at least determine the eventual size of the offspring. This is not so. There have been instances of a

Dachshund breeding a Setter bitch; once, this was accomplished through an Anchor wire fence. I have seen the results of a Basset-German Shepherd cross. And, in my own kennels, a 26-inch, one hundred pound Shepherd stud mated with an under 13-inch Beagle bitch. She was so small that, when they were tied, only the tips of her front toes touched the ground.

You can probably acquire a mongrel pup for little or nothing, while a purebred will carry a price tag in keeping with his quality. But don't allow this initial outlay to deter you from purchasing the purebred, registered puppy. Remember that it will cost you just as much for feeding, keeping and veterinary fees for the mongrel as for the registered pup during its lifetime, a sum far in excess of any initial purchase price. And, during the lifetime of your dog, you will have an animal in

Most mongrels are of unknown, questionable backgrounds and the result of an unplanned breeding.

which you can take pride as you can with all fine things. Actually, if you amortize the cost of your dog over his average lifespan you will find that you can purchase the love and loyalty of a fine animal, the result of countless generations of thoughtful breeding.

Many pedigreed puppies in the pet category can be bought at a reasonable price. Mongrels can often be acquired free of charge, since the owner wants to be rid of them. Crossbreds can be bought for much less, and sometimes these come as gifts, too. Remember this though, the pup you get for little or nothing has

One of the benefits of buying a mongrel puppy is that one can be purchased for little or no charge. However, there are no registration papers nor any guarantee that the dog is free of diseases or other health problems that can be very costly in the future.

Even though a mongrel may be acquired free of charge, the savings you have made cannot compare to the value placed on the time and energy spent in the breeding of a purebred puppy.

probably had no protection from distemper and other dog diseases. It will, undoubtedly, be infested with various canine worm forms and may become ill and a burden and expense to you.

The well-bred puppy represents an investment of time and money to the breeder and the sale price is a return on his investment. Consequently he will give the pup every care so that, when sold, it will not be brought back to him due to illness and he will therefore not have to return the purchase price or replace the puppy, both of which would constitute a monetary loss to him.

# CHOOSING YOUR PUPPY

Let us now assume that you have decided upon the specific breed of dog you want, the purpose to which the adult dog will be put, and the place where the puppy will be purchased. At this point there are two important factors that must be thoroughly checked before you make your final selection of the puppy that you will take home. First, be sure the puppy is a healthy one; second, be positive that he has a good disposition.

A puppy should be outgoing and friendly, willing, even eager, to be handled. He should come to you directly without hesitation, wag his tail and lick your face when picked up in your arms. Even if you contemplate training him to be a guard dog he should still exhibit boldness and friendliness. It is this kind of temperament that lends itself to training of any kind for it is directly associated with willingness, intelligence, confidence in his surroundings and a normal approach to any task.

**The puppy you choose should be healthy, outgoing, friendly, and willing to be handled.**

Beware of the puppy who sits in a corner all by himself, or the one who runs or backs away from your extended hand. Don't allow pity for the little fellow with the "hangdog" expression override your good common sense. The pup who doesn't act in a friendly, outgoing manner is not mentally sound and will probably never be at ease in any environment.

Shy puppies can develop into fearbiters. A fearbiter is an animal whose fear blankets all other considerations. Such a dog will, when frightened, snap and bite wildly in an attempt to protect itself from a danger that doesn't exist except in its own fearful and confused mind. Remember that in dogs we find mental patterns quite similar to those of humans. There are dog gangsters, bullies, bluffs, swaggers and timid souls; there are morons, geniuses and animals that are mentally ill in many and varied categories. You don't want your puppy to be a canine juvenile delinquent, so be careful when you make your selection. Bring home a normal, happy, mentally healthy puppy that will bring you pleasure and companionship rather than aggravation and trouble.

Make sure that the puppy's eyes are bright, he's lively, his skin is loose and pliable and his coat is soft and shiny. He should be fat and frisky, but not obviously pot-bellied. The latter is an indication of worms. Coughing, runny eyes or nose and a tendency to drag his hind end on the ground, particularly after having relieved

A child and a puppy make a perfect pair. Be sure to bring home a puppy that will bring you and your family pleasure and companionship rather than aggravation and trouble.

himself, also indicate worms. A dull, dry coat, lackluster attitude and discharge of eyes and nose are the signs of beginning illness.

If you find a puppy with the temperament you want and who

seems healthy and full of life, be sure to ask the seller when he was last wormed, what type of worms were evident, if he has had inoculations or vaccinations, what they were for and if and when they are to be continued.

Should you select a male puppy be sure that both testicles have descended into the scrotum. Retained testicles that stay in the body cavity and do not come down (called orchidism; monorchidism when one is retained in the body, cryptorchidism when both have failed to descend) can become cancerous when the dog has matured. Retained testicles also can cause deviation in temperament.

In general, when selecting a puppy, look for a healthy, happy animal who is normal in every way and is typical of his breed in coat, color and temperament. If he is a purebred, make sure you get both pedigree and registration papers with him. Don't let the breeder "con" you into paying more for the same puppy if pedigree and registration papers are supplied. If the seller does

With several breeds, such as the Boxer, you have the option of ear cropping. Cropping the ears is performed not only for aesthetic purposes but for health reasons as well.

demand an extra fee to supply such papers you would be wise to seek a puppy elsewhere, since this is one sign of an unscrupulous dealer.

## OTHER EXPENSES

With the purchase price come other expenses that you must consider if you are interested in certain breeds. If the puppy is a terrier or spaniel his tail should have been docked when he was about six days old. If it hasn't, then you will have to add the cost of docking to your purchase price. Unless he is a member of a very few breeds whose standards call for dewclaws (extra toes on the hind feet), these unsightly appendages should have been

removed in his first few days of life. If they haven't, it will be up to you to have them removed, another expense. Doberman Pinschers, Great Danes, Boxers, Schnauzers, and many other breeds have their ears cropped. If you select a puppy of any of these breeds it will cost you a little to get this done plus a good deal of trouble and time in caring for the ears after cropping.

Don't buy expensive furnishings for the puppy such as collars, leashes, bed, etc., that he will shortly outgrow. Consider his full growth when purchasing accessories of quality. Be sure, however, that what you do buy for him is durable, safe and strong.

Toys that squeak or click are fun for both you and your puppy, but be careful because your puppy can remove the squeaky device and choke on it. Your puppy will also need safe and effective chew devices to satisfy his chewing needs. The safest and most provenly effective canine chew products are the Nylabone® and Gumabone® pacifiers. These chewing devices are made of annealed nylon and heat treated polymers respectively and are clinically proven to prevent accumulation of tartar and plaque on the dog's teeth. If your puppy is kept in a run where he defecates, don't give him any toys or chew devices. They will, in the process of play, come in contact with stools left by the pup and become contaminated with worm eggs, which will be ingested by the puppy and cause reinfestation of worms.

## MALE OR FEMALE?

Another vital question when

All puppies need something to satisfy their need to chew. Be sure to provide your puppy with a proper, safe chewing device such as a Nylabone®.

selecting a puppy is, "Which sex shall I choose?" Most people who have made dogs either their vocation or their hobby will recommend that you purchase a female. The buyer's immediate reaction is a mental picture on wide screen depicting a bitch coming home followed by a belligerent mob of non-descript and dirty male dogs. The worry of keeping a bitch in season in close confinement, or the cost of kenneling her at your veterinarian's or a commercial kennel until her mating cycle has passed, looms big to the neophyte dog owner.

There is also the possibility that the owner of a female may have to raise an unwanted litter if the bitch is accidentally bred. There are also the not infrequent diseases of the reproductive tract to which the female is prone; and these must be taken into consideration.

All these problems are certainly very real, but are overshadowed by the many virtues inherent in the female for the canine species.

Aside from these drawback females have much to recommend them. They are generally quieter and cleaner than males. The fact that they squat while urinating will keep

Once you have chosen a particular breed, the next decision you must make is whether to buy a male or female. Females are often recommended as housepets because they are generally quieter, cleaner and more affectionate than males.

flowers and shrubs around the house from being urine-burned. They are frequently more easily housebroken than the male, and they generally exhibit a greater degree of affection and love for the family.

If you keep your bitch whole and do not spay her, another important factor to be considered is the female's basic reason for being, in nature's scheme of things, and the effect this can have on your youngsters. There is no better way to teach children the facts of life than through the agency of a bred and whelping bitch. The reasons for the specific breeding (the betterment of the breed), the act itself and the subsequent whelping and care of puppies by the bitch, if properly handled by the parents, can give your children an understanding of sex swept clean of any suggestion of evil. The fumbling approach to the old "birds and bees" story by an embarrassed parent will no longer be necessary.

A bitch can, of course, be spayed, and will then be no problem at all. In fact, if you want a dog to be only a family pet, a spayed bitch is the perfect animal. Remember, though, that once she has been altered there is no turning back. I mention this because I have frequently seen people buy a bitch puppy for a pet, have her spayed, then later become interested in the breed, want to

house or at your veterinarian's kennel, for prowling canine Casanovas are as practiced at getting to a female at the right time as was their human counterpart.

It can be said with conviction that male dogs are constantly in heat instead of only twice a year as in the

Since males have a tendency to roam, it is suggested that you have your male puppy neutered if you do not intend to breed.

show and breed and come to realize, when it is too late, that the bitch they bought for a pet and spayed could have been valuable in their breeding program.

Spaying is a simple operation, neither costly to the owner or painful to the dog. It should not be done at too early an age. It is best to wait until the pup is about to have her first period. If spayed too early in life, females have a tendency to become lazy and fat and will lose their femininity of form and will become more male-like and coarser in head and structure.

If you buy a female and decide not to spay her, remember that she will come in heat about twice a year and you must protect her from itinerant male dogs. It is best to keep her strictly confined in the

case of the bitch. They will, like all unattached males regardless of species, roam their habitat seeking the joys of love. Often they will be lost for days following the scent of a delectable female, and return home tired, shame-faced and moth-eaten, looking for all the world like Bowery bums. Males, even those that are thoroughly housebroken, will frequently urinate on walls and furniture if a bitch in heat has been in the room.

Males are more aggressive than bitches, and because of this factor, usually make better guard dogs. They mature into larger and generally more impressive examples of their individual breed than do females. Since they lift their leg when urinating, they can do damage to bushes and other growing vegetation on your (and your neighbor's) land.

# BRINGING THE PUPPY HOME

Before you bring your puppy home you should be prepared for his arrival. There are many items that you will need for him. You must also be prepared for the trip from the seller's place of business to your home. This will require a crate big enough for the puppy to be put into and roomy enough to allow him to move about. Lots of newspaper for the bottom of the box and any accidents and a few pieces of clean cloth are also necessary. You can assume, especially if the trip home is to be a long one, that the pup will become carsick and vomit. Clean newspaper and a cloth to wipe the puppy's mouth and any body areas that become soiled will immediately be needed. By keeping the pup in a crate the accident will not happen while being held on the lap of one of your family. Sometimes a lot of attention during the trip will keep him so occupied that he will not vomit, particularly if he had not been fed immediately prior to the trip.

A number of preparations must be made prior to your puppy's arrival, including transporting him home. There is certainly a safer alternative to letting him ride in the passenger seat.

**PREPARING FOR THE NEW PUPPY**

Preparations for the puppy's arrival must include a bed, a collar and leash, two pans, one for food and the other for water and complete agreement between the members of your family as to where the puppy will sleep and where he will be kept.

Collar, leash, bed and pans can be expensive or inexpensive, according to your taste and your pocketbook. To the puppy the quality and cost of these items couldn't matter less. Just remember that the pup will grow out of all of them in a short time unless, in buying the bed and pans, you have taken this into consideration. Durability should be the owner's aim when buying these items.

A thin, flat or rolled collar is best. Wide, heavy collars cut the neck hair especially in longer coated breeds, and mar the symmetry of the neckline.

The items mentioned above are basic essentials. You will also need a comb and brush suitable for the type of coat your puppy wears, nail clippers, a good flea spray, dog soap and a dry cleanser. Your puppy will also need something to chew on. For puppies, the Gumabone® products are probably best, due to their softer composition. Puppies should never be given an old shoe, sock or household object as a chew device: not only can these be dangerous but they can also confuse the puppy about appropriate objects to chew. Other essentials are a large supply of newspapers, a good rug cleaner and a vast amount of patience and self-control. Armed with these necessities you are ready to face the future as a bonafide dog owner.

A well-sized crate should be your first purchase before obtaining your puppy. Besides safe transportation, the crate provides a quiet place where your puppy can rest. Be sure to buy a crate that is big enough to house your puppy when he matures into a full-sized dog.

Your new puppy (or puppies) will need a soft, comfortable place to sleep. Your local pet shop has a wide variety of beds in all shapes, sizes, and colors to fit your particular puppy's needs.

Pet shops sell fuzzy toys that your puppy will enjoy. Careful supervison is mandatory in case your puppy tears it open and attempts to eat the filling.

## SLEEPING ACCOMMODATIONS

Decide where the puppy will sleep and make sure the location isn't drafty or near a radiator. Buy or borrow from your children, a stuffed animal of some kind approximately the size of the puppy, and bring it with you when you go to buy your pup. Rub this stuffed monstrosity in the kennel bed and over your puppy's littermates so that it is permeated with familiar odors. When you remove him from his dam and his brothers and sisters and put him in a strange environment, he will be lonely and bewildered the first night. If he can cuddle up to the pseudo-animal, alive with familiar scents, it might keep him quiet and content. This will save you and your family from a sleepless night listening to forlorn howls and wondering why you were insane enough to even think of buying a dog in the first place. A ticking clock sometimes also keeps a puppy quiet that first, vital night.

A polyurethane toy, such as this Gumabone® Frisbee®*, is a safe and entertaining choice for young Rottweilers.
*The trademark Frisbee is used under license from Mattel, Inc., California, USA

It happens, all too frequently, that one of the family finally gives in to the mournful wails of the lonely puppy and takes him to their own bed. This is a mistake. A habit pattern might be formed that will be hard to break; and it will be more difficult later to teach the pup that he must be quiet at night and sleep in his own quarters.

diet is not essentially correct, you can introduce the new diet gradually. Incorporate it into the puppy's diet by using larger portions of the new food with each feeding until the earlier diet has been eliminated entirely. By employing this method you will not upset a puppy brought into new surroundings through an abrupt dietary change.

**Your new puppy is used to sleeping with his littermates. Therefore, the first few nights in his new home may be difficult and frightening. Be sensitive and understanding with your new housemate.**

**OTHER PREPARATIONS**

Find out from the seller what the puppy has been fed. Incidentally, be sure that the youngster is completely weaned, and eating on his own, before you buy. When you first bring your puppy home, make sure you have a supply of the food and supplements the seller used so that you can feed him in the same manner. If you decide this initial

Because the unaccustomed movement of your car during travel may have upset him, do not attempt to feed him for a short time after arrival at his new home. Give his stomach a chance to settle.

**INTRODUCTION TO THE NEW HOME**

Introduce you new puppy to his bed, his quarters and your family. Let him run and sniff and get

Your new puppy should become acquainted with everyone in his new home, including the family cat.

acquainted with everyone and everything. Both the puppy and your family, especially the children, will be excited by this change in their lives. But remember that this is a canine baby who needs lots of rest and sleep just as all babies do. It is your job to see that he gets it, although it may be a difficult assignment when there are children in the family. The children are to be made to realize that the puppy must have his necessary rest and sleep and that puppy playtime must come in between these periods. As the puppy grows older, his naps will grow shorter until eventually he will be more than a match for even the unbounding energy of the children.

## HANDLING THE PUPPY

You, and especially your children, should know the proper way to handle the new puppy. Many authorities claim that there is no one good way to handle a puppy and that they are so pliable that they can't be readily harmed by improper handling or picking up. This assumption is based on watching bitches pick their pups up by the skin of the neck or even with the pup's head in their mouth, when transporting them from one place to another. I cannot go along with the theory that if the mother carries the puppies in this manner it is the best way. The bitch can't carry them in any other manner than with her mouth and teeth, so she does. I am sure that if she had

**Young children must be instructed on the proper way to handle the new puppy.**

hands, she would find a much better way to carry her progeny.

The best way to pick up and carry a puppy is by using your hands to support his distributed weight. Put one hand under his chest between his forelegs and the other hand between his hindlegs. In this way you can pick him up and carry him without hurting him. It is a good thing to teach a child how to carry a puppy rather than to see very young children pick a puppy up by an ear or a leg. Such instruction is good for the child and certainly good for the puppy.

Puppies are cuddlesome tykes and the tendency is to hug them constantly. But, this constant close association with the human body causes a puppy to become a coddler and robs him of the independence a puppy needs to develop into a dependable adult. A good way to train your puppy for proper handling comes during the grooming period. Stand him on a box or some other object of convenient height and hold him at arm's length, standing up on all his four legs, while you groom him. Teach him to stand

As adorably cuddly a puppy may be, family members must understand that the growing puppy also needs his space. Puppies that are constantly coddled can become too attached to the person and become overly dependent.

ready while you comb and brush him. This is an easy approach to the more stringent training that comes later. Pups that are constantly cuddled and held close become "leaners" and are difficult to pry loose from their owners when they are taken to the veterinarian for treatment, or for any other purpose.

Unless you plan to have your dog constantly with you, in the house and wherever you go, it is best to build a house and run for him in your backyard. You will know then that your puppy is safe when you are away from the house, and that he is enjoying the sun and fresh air. This arrangement also obviates the necessity of taking him out on a leash for long walks, though frequently "walking the dog" is more beneficial to the owner than the dog because it is the only exercise the owner gets. Having a run of his own also helps in developing independence in the dog.

The chore of housebreaking is one of the biggest jobs for the new puppy owner. In many cases people who want a puppy decide not to have one because they dream up the housebreaking bug-a-boo into a monster beyond its true proportions.

If you wish to housebreak your puppy quickly and easily (and who doesn't?) there are several facts you should know and remember. First, you the owner, must know and recognize the symptoms indicating that the puppy is about to heed the call of nature. Second, you must be aware of the conditions under which the puppy was kept before you brought him home. The underfoot materials the puppy knew previously when he found it necessary to excrete are important for you to know about. Last, but not least, you must be prompt and consistent in your training regime.

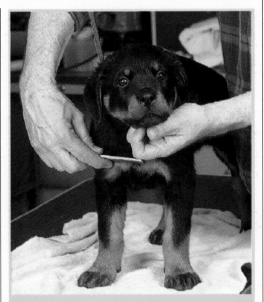

A good way to train your puppy for proper handling is during a grooming session. Teach him to stand ready on all four legs while you comb and brush him.

Housebreaking is one of the biggest jobs for the new puppy owner. One of the factors you should be aware of is the type of underfooting your puppy eliminated on before you brought him home. Many breeders use newspaper because it is cheap, absorbent, and easy to dispose.

# VACCINATIONS

For the continued health of your dog, owners must attend to vaccinations regularly. Your veterinarian can recommend a vaccination schedule appropriate for your dog taking into consideration the factors of climate and geography. The basic vaccinations to protect your dog

first recognized in 1978. Targeting the small intestine, parvo affects the stomach and diarrhea and vomiting (with blood) are clinical signs. Although the dog can pass the infection to other dogs within three days of infection, the initial signs, which include lethargy and depression, don't display

There are many diseases that a young puppy can acquire if preventative measures are not taken. Your growing puppy must rely on you for his vaccinations and continued health.

are: parvovirus, distemper, hepatitis, leptospirosis, adenovirus, parainfluenza, coronavirus, bordetella, tracheobronchitis (kennel cough), Lyme disease and rabies.

Parvovirus is a highly contagious, dog-specific disease,

themselves until four to seven days. When affecting puppies under four weeks of age, the heart muscle is frequently attacked. When the heart is affected, the puppies exhibit difficulty in breathing and experience crying and foaming at the nose and mouth.

Distemper, related to human measles, is an airborne virus that spreads in the blood and ultimately in the nervous system and epithelial tissues. Young dogs or dogs with weak immune systems can develop encephalomyelitis (brain disease) from the distemper infection. Such dogs experience seizures, general weakness and rigidity, as well as "hardpad". Since

Hepatitis mainly affects the liver and is caused by canine adenovirus type I. Highly infectious, hepatitis often affects dogs nine to 12 months of age. Initially the virus localizes in the dog's tonsils and then disperses to the liver, kidney and eyes. Generally speaking the dog's immune system is capable of combating this virus. Canine infectious hepatitis affects dogs

## VACCINATION SCHEDULE

| Age | Vaccination |
|---|---|
| 6-8 weeks | Initial canine distemper, canine hepatitis, tracheobronchitis, canine parvovirus as well as initial leptospirosis vaccination. |
| 10-12 weeks | Second vaccination for all given at 6-8 weeks. Initial rabies and initial Lyme disease to be given at this time. |
| 14-16 weeks | Third vaccination for all given at 6-8 and 10-12 weeks. Re-vaccinate annually, hereafter. Second rabies and second Lyme disease to be given at this time, and then re-vaccinated annually. |

distemper is largely incurable, prevention through vaccination is vitally important. Puppies should be vaccinated at six to eight weeks of age, with boosters at ten to 12 weeks. Older puppies (16 weeks and older) who are unvaccinated should receive no fewer than two vaccinations at three- to four- week intervals.

whose systems cannot fight off the adenovirus. Affected dogs have fever, abdominal pains, bruising on mucous membranes and gums, and experience coma and convulsions. Prevention of hepatitis exists only through vaccination at eight to ten weeks of age and then boosters three or four weeks later, then annually.

**Tall grasses and weeds are prime habitats for a number of parasites. Be sure to brush your puppy thoroughly after spending time in such areas.**

Leptospirosis is a bacterium-related disease, often spread by rodents. The organisms that spread leptospirosis enter through the mucous membrane and spread to the internal organs via the bloodstream. It can be passed through the dog's urine. Leptospirosis does not affect young dogs as consistently as the other viruses; it is reportedly regional in distribution and somewhat dependent on the immunostatus of the dog. Fever, inappetence, vomiting, dehydration, hemorrhage, kidney and eye disease can result in moderate cases.

Bordetella, called canine cough, causes a persistent hacking cough in dogs and is very contagious. Bordetella involves a virus and a bacteria: parainfluenza is the most common virus implicated;

*Bordetella bronchiseptica,* the bacterium. Bronchitis and pneumonia result in less than 20 percent of the cases, and most dogs recover from the condition within a week to four weeks. Non-prescription medicines can help relieve the hacking cough, though nothing can cure the condition before it's run its course. Vaccination cannot guarantee protection from canine cough, but it does ward off the most common virus responsible for the condition.

Lyme disease (also called borreliosis), although known since for decades, was only first diagnosed in dogs in 1984. Lyme disease can affect cats, cattle, and horses, but especially people. In the U.S., the disease is transmitted by two ticks carrying the *Borrelia burgdorferi* organism: the deer tick (*Ixodes scapularis*) and the western black-legged tick (*Ixodes pacificus*), the latter primarily affects reptiles. In Europe, *Ixodes ricinus* is responsible for spreading Lyme. The disease causes lameness, fever, joint swelling, inappetence, and lethargy. Removal of ticks from the dog's coat can help reduce the chances of Lyme, though not as much as avoiding heavily wooded areas where the dog is most likely to contract ticks. A vaccination is available, though has not been proven to protect dogs from all strains of the organism that causes the disease.

Rabies is passed to dogs and people through wildlife: in North America, principally through the skunk, fox and raccoon; the bat is

**Lyme disease is carried by two types of ticks and affects both dogs and humans. The prevention from this dangerous illness is to avoid heavily wooded areas, where Lyme-carrying ticks make their home.**

not the culprit it was once thought to be. Likewise, the common image of the rabid dog foaming at the mouth with every hair on end is unlikely the truest scenario. A rabid dog exhibits difficulty eating, salivates much and has spells of paralysis and awkwardness. Before a dog reaches this final state, it may experience anxiety, personality changes, irritability and more aggressiveness than is usual. Vaccinations are strongly recommended as affected dogs are too dangerous to manage and are commonly euthanized. Puppies are generally vaccinated at 12 weeks of age, and then annually. Although rabies is on the decline in the world community, tens of thousands of humans die each year from rabies-related incidents.

# HOUSEBREAKING THE PUPPY

Puppies will urinate very soon after drinking water, and they will defecate within a half hour after eating. Watch the pup carefully and you will soon become aware of the warning signs and movements that precede evacuation. When you see these signs, pick the pup up immediately and rush him to the place that you have assigned for these duties, indoor or out.

When the pup, by accident or design, goes where you want him to, praise him extravagantly, letting him know how pleased you are with his deportment. Should he make a mistake (and he frequently will), scold him, using your voice and its tone to impart to him your displeasure at his conduct. The simple word, "No," used correctly, is adequate. Praise can be conveyed by the words, "Good boy," or "Good girl." Repeat oral admonition or praise several times using your tone of voice to convey your feelings.

Puppies raised on an earth surface are the easiest to housebreak. Simply take the puppy to the backyard when he is ready and, feeling the familiar ground underfoot, he will quickly eliminate.

Pups raised in earth-surfaced runs are the most easily housebroken. Simply take them out to the backyard when they are ready and, feeling familiar texture underfoot, they will readily oblige.

The owner of a pup raised on an earth surface is lucky, since this eliminates one important step in the housebreaking routine. The object of most owners, other than a few owners of toy dogs, is to eventually train their dogs to go outside and not in the house at all. But, with the paper-trained puppy, there must be a transition from inside to outside. To accomplish this, the paper must be moved outside and the puppy taken outdoors and brought to it. At first the paper should have been soiled by the puppy, and then taken outdoors. The pup, brought to the paper outside then, by scent, knows what it is for. Stones, on the four

When trained to do his business outdoors, your puppy will likely choose a favorite spot in the yard and use it regularly.

corners, can be used to anchor the paper to the ground. Within a short time the puppy, brought to the paper, will generally repeat the same performance he has been accustomed to doing in the house.

To reach the point where the puppy no longer needs the paper and will use the Great Outdoors, you must gradually decrease the size of the paper on the ground for his use, until only the bare earth or grass remains. When this time comes your puppy should be fully housebroken. Congratulations!

Some smaller breeds of dogs are sometimes raised in wire-bottom pens and when the puppy defecates, his stool drops through the wire to the ground below. This is a method designed to aid in keeping puppies from reinfesting themselves with worms or coccidiosis. But, since the pup is accustomed to wire under his feet when he heeds the call of nature, you had better not buy him if your home is equipped with floor grates for central heating or hot air heat, or you will have a problem. The pup will seek this grating every time he feels the need to relieve himself. The best way to solve this problem is to make very sure you catch him before he errs and bring him to the spot you have selected.

If you find it necessary to go out and leave the puppy alone in the house for any period of time, it is best to confine him to a limited area, which also includes the paper.

Face the problem of housebreaking with aplomb, not with grimness. Laugh off the puddles, piddles and odors, and, if

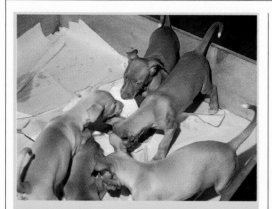

Paper training is easy if your puppy's whelping box was lined with paper. He will recognize and prefer the same material he eliminated on since birth.

you are determined and thorough, you will soon be through with them and can blithely congratulate yourself and your pup on a job well done.

## PAPER TRAINING

Paper training a puppy is easy if the youngster's nest had previously been of paper. Whatever material he had under his feet in the nest before you brought him home will have a great deal to do with the rapidity with which he is housebroken. The puppy will inadvertently prefer to go on the same kind of material that he has felt underfoot and used for this purpose since he was born. He has been conditioned to do this. Therefore, if the surface under his baby feet supplied by the breeder had been paper, he will be readily paper trained.

Place the paper in a specific place, the best place being a corner of the bathroom, though many people prefer a corner of the

kitchen instead. When you notice the signs that indicate that he is about to go, take him to the paper and hold him there until he does. Then praise him and tell him what a fine individual he is. A puppy will almost always go after he's had a nap and awakens. Take him immediately after awakening to the paper and you will generally have success. Be consistent, never allow him to go any other place in the house without scolding him and marching him to the paper. In this way you will condition the puppy to run to the specific place you want him to go, and use the paper supplied for him. Soon, both of you will take pride in his intelligent cooperation.

When you recognize the signs that your puppy is about to go, take him to the paper and hold him there until he does. Praise him excessively once he goes to reinforce training.

# GROOMING

Grooming should be a pleasant experience and a time of silent and delightful communication between you and your dog. Try to find the time to groom your puppy once every day. It should take only a few minutes of your time, except during the season of shedding. By removing dead hair, dust and skin scales in the daily grooming, you keep your pup's coat glossy and his appearance neat. This kind of daily grooming also eliminates the necessity of frequent bathings. For ordinary grooming use a metal comb with a handle. A comb of this sort permits you to dig below the surface of the outer coat. Be careful not to irritate the skin or pull out the undercoat. After combing thoroughly, go over the dog with a stiff-bristled brush. During the shedding season, a coarse-toothed hacksaw blade pulled through the coat is handy for removing loose hair below the

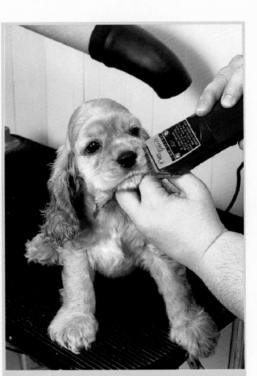

Grooming should be a pleasant experience and a time to bond with your puppy.

coat surface. During the grooming procedure, beginning skin disease can be seen and nipped in the bud.

BATHING

You may bathe your puppy any time you think it necessary, as long as you do not think this too frequently. Be careful in chilly weather to bathe him in a warm room and make sure he is completely dry before you allow him to venture out into the cold outdoors. When you bathe your dog, you soak him down to the skin and remove the protective oils from his coat. When a dog is exposed to rain and snow, the dampness is shed by the outer coat and kept from his skin by his undercoat. Therefore he is not likely to be affected by natural seasonal conditions. Be careful, however, that he is not exposed to these same conditions directly after a bath, as there is danger of his contracting a cold. During the time of shedding, a bath once a week is not too often if the weather is warm. It helps to remove loose hair and skin scales, as does the grooming that should follow the bath when the dog is completely dry. When bathing, rub the lather in strongly down to the skin, being careful not to get soap in the dog's eyes. Cover every inch of him with heavy lather, rub it in, scrape the excess off with your hands, rinse and dry thoroughly, then walk him in the sun until he is ready for

are useful in keeping dogs clean and odorless.

There are many dog people who do not believe in frequent bathing because it tends to remove the oil from the dog's coat and can result in dry skin, dandruff, and itchy skin. If you are one of these people and wish to keep your puppy clean and fresh-looking without fully bathing him, you can do so by employing the following procedure. First, fill a pail with lukewarm

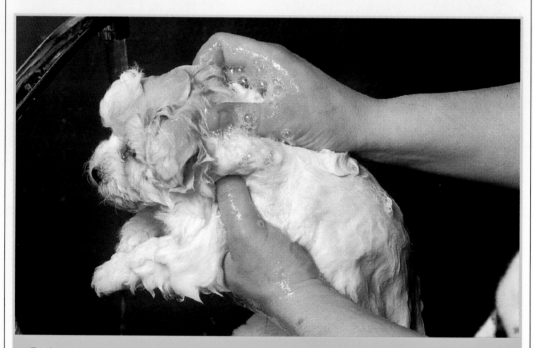

**Bathe your puppy as often as you deem necessary. To prevent the catching of a cold, be sure that both the water and the air are warm, and dry your puppy thoroughly when finished.**

grooming. There are paste soaps available that require no rinsing, making the bathing of your pup that much easier, or you may wish to use liquid detergents manufactured specifically for canine bathing. Prepared canned lathers, as well as dry shampoos, are all available at pet shops and

water and swish a bar of a bland cosmetic soap through the water until it is slightly cloudy. Dip a large towel in the water and throw it over your puppy's back in much the same manner as a drying blanket is draped over a horse. Begin rubbing the moisture through your puppy's coat from

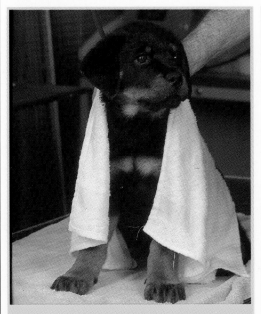

Be sure to throroughly dry your puppy after bathing. Use a soft towel and rub briskly to remove all moisture from his coat.

behind his ears down to his neck, back, croup, etc., until you have rubbed him all over. Then rinse the towel in fresh water, wring it out, and repeat the procedure until the first liquid application has been completely removed. Following this, rub the dog down briskly with a dry towel, comb him in the direction of the lay of his coat and allow him to dry in the sun if possible. Do not permit him to roll in the dirt or earth, a habit which seems to be the particular delight of most dogs after bathing or grooming.

If your pup has walked in tar, which you find you cannot remove by bathing, you can remove it with kerosene. The kerosene should *quickly* be removed with strong soap and water so it does not burn

Groom your puppy on a daily basis, using a metal comb with a handle. This type of comb allows you to dig below the surface of the outer coat.

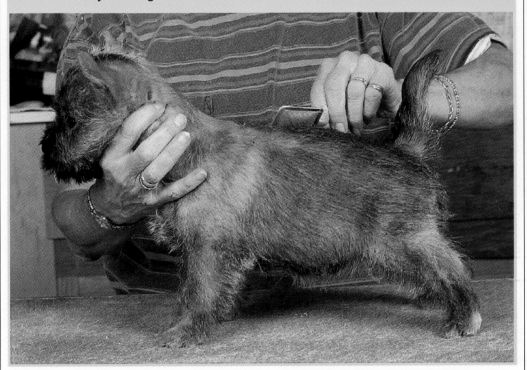

and irritate the skin. Paint can be washed off with turpentine, which must also quickly be removed for the same reasons. Some synthetic paints, lacquer and other like preparations, which are thinned with alcohol, can be removed by the same vehicle. If the paint (oil base) is close to the skin, linseed oil will dissolve it without irritation. Should your puppy engage in a tete-a-tete with a skunk, wash him immediately (if you can get near him) with soap and hot water, or soak him with tomato juice if you can find enough available, then walk him in the hot sun. The odor evaporates most quickly under heat.

A box of cotton swabs, which are manufactured under various brand names, are excellent for cleaning your puppy's ears. There are many ear-cleansing solutions available at your local pet shop. Drop an ear-cleansing solution into the ear (according to the directions on the bottle) to dissolve dirt and wax, then swab the ear clean. Surplus liquid will quickly evaporate.

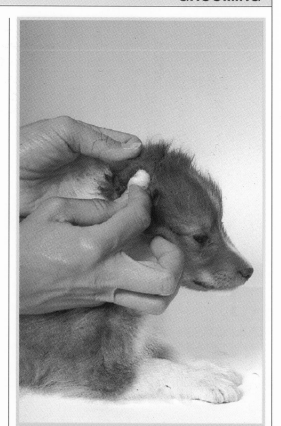

When grooming your puppy, don't neglect the ears. Apply a good ear cleasning solution (available at your pet shop) and wipe away all dirt and wax with cotton balls or swabs.

Begin grooming sessions as early as possible to accustom your puppy to being handled and to prevent future problems.

## CARE OF NAILS

Keep your puppy's nails trimmed short. Overgrown nails cause lameness, foot ailments, spread toes, hare feet and runs in women's stockings. If your dog does a great deal of walking on cement, nail growth is often kept under control naturally by wearing off on the cement surface. Some dogs seem to possess a

If you cut too deeply, you will cause bleeding. A flashlight held under the nail will enable you to see the dark area of the blood line, known as the quick, so you can avoid cutting into it. If you should cut the quick, don't be overly alarmed, simply keep the dog quiet until the severed capillaries close and the bleeding stops. A styptic pencil applied to

Short-coated breeds of dog, such as the Beagle, require very little grooming. A daily brushing with a short-bristle brush or a hound glove will keep your puppy's coat looking shiny and healthy.

genetic factor for short nails that never need trimming, but the majority need nail care. To accomplish this task with the least possible trouble, use a nail cutter specifically designed to trim canine nails and cut away only the horny dead section of the nail.

the bleeding nail helps to hurry coagulation. After you have cut the nails, file them smooth with the use of an ordinary nail file. File from above with a downward, rounding stroke. If a nail has bled from trimming, do not file it for at least 24 hours.

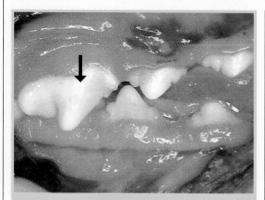

In a scientific study, this shows a dog's tooth (arrow) while being maintained by Gumabone® chewing.

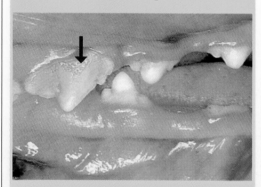

The Gumabone® was taken away and in 30 days the tooth was almost completely covered with plaque and tartar.

## ALL DOGS NEED TO CHEW

Puppies and young dogs need something with resistance to chew on while their teeth and jaws are developing—for cutting the puppy teeth, to induce growth of the permanent teeth under the puppy teeth, to assist in getting rid of the puppy teeth at the proper time, to help the permanent teeth through the gums, to ensure normal jaw development and to settle the permanent teeth solidly in the jaws.

The adult dog's desire to chew stems from the instinct for tooth cleaning, gum massage and jaw exercise—plus the need for an outlet

for periodic doggie tensions.

This is why dogs, especially puppies and young dogs, will often destroy property worth hundreds of dollars when their chewing instinct is not diverted from their owner's possessions. And this is why you should provide your dog with something to chew—something that has the necessary functional qualities, is desirable from the dog's viewpoint and is safe for your dog.

It is very important that dogs not be permitted to chew on anything they can break or on any indigestible thing from which they can bite sizable chunks. Sharp pieces, such

The nylon tug toy is actually a dental floss. You grab one end and let your puppy tug on the other as it slowly slips through his teeth since nylon is self-lubricating (slippery). Do NOT use cotton rope tug toys as cotton is orgainc and rots. It is also weak and easily loses strands which are indigestible should the puppy swallow them.

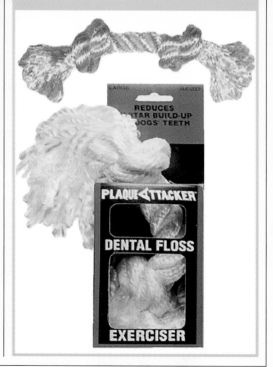

as from a bone which can be broken by a dog, may pierce the intestinal wall and kill. Indigestible things that can be bitten off in chunks, such as from shoes or rubber or plastic toys, may cause an intestinal stoppage (if not regurgitated) and bring painful death, unless surgery is promptly performed.

Strong natural bones, such as 4- to 8-inch lengths of round shin increases until maturity. This means that a growing dog may break one of the smaller bones at any time, swallow the pieces and die painfully before you realize what is wrong.

All hard natural bones are very abrasive. If your dog is an avid chewer, natural bones may wear away his teeth prematurely; hence, they then should be taken away from your dog when the

**Two Akita puppies have a fun and healthy time tugging a Plaque Attacker™. Playing with the tug toy is a great way for puppies to relieve stress while cleaning their teeth at the same time.**

bone from mature beef—either the kind you can get from a butcher or one of the variety available commercially in pet stores—may serve your dog's teething needs if his mouth is large enough to handle them effectively. You may be tempted to give your puppy a smaller bone and he may not be able to break it when you do, but puppies grow rapidly and the power of their jaws constantly teething purposes have been served. The badly worn, and usually painful, teeth of many mature dogs can be traced to excessive chewing on natural bones.

Contrary to popular belief, knuckle bones that can be chewed up and swallowed by the dog provide little, if any, usable calcium or other nutriment. They do, however, disturb the digestion

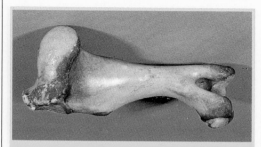

Pet shops sell real bones which have been colored, cooked, dyed or served natural. Some of the bones are huge, but they usually are easily destroyed by puppies and become very dangerous.

of most dogs and cause them to vomit the nourishing food they need.

Dried rawhide products of various types, shapes, sizes, and prices are available on the market and have become quite popular. However, they don't serve the primary chewing functions very well; they are a bit messy when wet from mouthing, and most dogs chew them up rather rapidly—but they have been considered safe for dogs until recently. Now, more and more incidents of death, and near death, by strangulation have been reported to be the results of partially swallowed chunks of

A chicken-flavored Gumabone® has tiny particles of chicken powder embedded in it to keep the puppy interested.

rawhide swelling in the throat. More recently, some veterinarians have been attributing cases of acute constipation to large pieces of incompletely digested rawhide in the intestine.

A new product, molded rawhide, is very safe. During the process, the rawhide is melted and then injection molded into the familiar dog shape. It is very hard and eagerly accepted by puppies and adult dogs. Don't confuse this with pressed rawhide, which is nothing

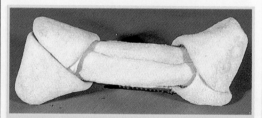

Rawhide is probably the best-selling dog chew. It can be dangerous and cause a dog to choke on it as it swells when wet. A molded, melted rawhide mixed with casein is available (though always scarce). This is the only suitable rawhide for puppies.

more than small strips of rawhide squeezed together.

The nylon bones, especially those with natural meat and bone fractions added, are probably the most complete, safe and economical answer to the chewing need. Dogs cannot break them or bite off sizable chunks; hence, they are completely safe—and being longer lasting than other things offered for the purpose, they are economical.

Hard chewing raises little bristle-like projections on the surface of the nylon bones—to provide effective interim tooth cleaning and

**Dogs can get a good dental workout as well as healthy protein. Choose a hard doggie treat such as Chooz®, made from cheese protein.**

Most pet shops have complete walls dedicated to safe pacifiers.

Start your puppy with the Puppy Bone from Nylabone®—it's designed to pacify the young dog and to enhance jaw development.

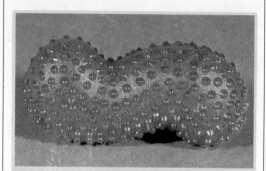

As your puppy grows, his teeth will become stronger. The Hercules has been designed with powerful chewers in mind. It is made of plastic polyurethane.

The Galileo is an extremely tough nylon pacifier. Its design is based upon original sketches by Galileo.

Raised dental tips on each dog bone works wonders with controlling plaque in puppies.

**Provide your puppy with a safe, functional device that will divert his chewing needs away from your valuable possessions. Nylabone® has a whole line of chew toys that your puppy will both enjoy and benefit from.**

vigorous gum massage, much in the same way your toothbrush does it for you. The little projections are raked off and swallowed in the form of thin shavings, but the chemistry of the nylon is such that they break down in the stomach fluids and pass through without effect.

The toughness of the nylon provides the strong chewing resistance needed for important jaw exercise and effectively aids teething functions, but there is no tooth wear because nylon is non-abrasive. Being inert, nylon does not support the growth of microorganisms; and it can be washed in soap and water or it can be sterilized by boiling or in an autoclave.

Nylabone® is highly recommended by veterinarians as a safe, healthy nylon bone that can't splinter or chip. Nylabone® is frizzled by the dog's chewing action, creating a toothbrush-like surface that cleanses the teeth and massages the gums. Nylabone® and Nylaball®, the only chew products made of flavor-impregnated solid nylon, are available in your local pet shop.

Nothing, however, substitutes for periodic professional attention for your dog's teeth and gums, not any more than your toothbrush can do that for you. Have your dog's teeth cleaned at least once a year by your veterinarian (twice a year is better) and he will be happier, healthier and far more pleasant to live with.

# EXERCISE

Exercise is one of the facets of canine care that is many times neglected by the owner. There should be some time set aside each day for play—a romp with a family member, perhaps. Not everyone is lucky enough to let his dog run through an open meadow, or along a sandy beach, but even a ten-minute walk in the fresh air will do. Whenever possible take a stroll to an empty lot, a playground or a nearby park and let your puppy run and jump and tone his body through aerobic

rural areas and allow their dogs the freedom of several acres can be sure that the animal is getting enough exercise by himself. Many a puppy will virtually exhaust himself chasing rabbits or other wild creatures native to the area, the bounding, running explosion of energy employed in the chase.

We have considered the elements of physical care, but we must not forget that your puppy needs mental care as well. His character and mental health need nourishment,

**Exercise is an important yet often neglected aspect of canine care. Allow your dog to take a nice stroll or run around an open area whenever possible.**

activity. You might also want to engage him in a simple game of fetch. Don't forget to "cool him down" afterwards with a rhythmic trot until his heart rate returns to normal. If the weather is exceptionally hot, it is best to skip the aerobic exercise for that day, or wait until the cool of the evening. Many owners who live in

grooming, and exercise, just as much as his physical being. Give him your companionship and understanding, teach him right from wrong, and treat him as you would a friend whom you enjoy associating with. This, too, is a part of his general care, and perhaps the most important part for both you and your dog.

Your puppy's mental and emotional well-being are just as important as his physical health. If you are fortunate, your puppies will have been socialized by a caring breeder.

# FEEDING YOUR PUPPY

Most puppies are weaned, and are eating from a dish by the time they are ready to go to their new home. If, for any reason, you happen to become the owner of a puppy not yet weaned (which would generally mean a pup under six to seven weeks of age), it will be your responsibility to teach him to eat by himself without benefit of his mother's milk. This may take a bit of doing. Common sense dictates, under such circumstances, that we should find the substitute for bitch's milk that most closely resembles the real thing. In consistency, a bitch's milk is like light cream, it contains between 9% and 13% butterfat and is acidified. The best substitute would be light cream to which has been added a dried baby milk product that has been enriched and acidified so that it more closely approaches the taste of bitch's milk than does plain cream or cow's milk.

This mixture warmed to body temperature, can be fed from a baby's bottle, nipple and all, or it can be fed from the palm of your cupped hand, urging the puppy to begin to lap its milk instead of sucking for it. You can then, within a day or two, train him to dish feeding. Fill a shallow saucer with the milk mixture and dip his underjaw and lips in the pan. Release him and he will begin to lick the milk adhering to his mouth. After repeating this action, he will begin to lick the milk adhering to his mouth. Soon he will begin to lap up milk by himself. A word of caution—do not force his muzzle so deeply into the milk that he sniffs some up his nose. This will cause him discomfort and he will struggle thus taking him longer to break into dish feeding.

Most puppies are eating out of a dish when they get to their new home. By this time, the puppy is ready to begin eating some solid food.

## ADDING SOLID FOODS

Once you have your puppy lapping out of a dish, it is time to begin adding solid food to his diet. Puppy meal is excellent food to add to the milk mixture. At first use very little so that the consistency isn't changed appreciably. Each day add a little more of the grain food until the meal has a porridge-like consistency. Begin to add a few drops of an oil product, such as cod liver oil, rich in necessary vitamins including K, the vitamin which is essential for puppy survival, to the meal.

Feed the puppy as much as he will eat of this mixture about six times a day. When he is six or milk, dried milk or warm water.

When the puppy has reached the age of three months, cut the number of meals to four. After five months the pup should be on a full, adult dry food.

The method just described is the easiest way to feed a dog, and be certain that he is being given a balanced diet. There is one mistake all too many puppy owners fall into; and that is the feeding of baby foods. To try to simulate human

If your new puppy has not yet been weaned, you will have to wean him using a mixture that closely resembles his mother's milk. This mixture should be warmed to body temperature and can be fed from a baby bottle.

seven weeks old, begin using about 10% melted fat in each meal (butter, oleo, bacon fat or melted beef suet). Cut the feedings to five at this time and make each meal larger. At eight or nine weeks you can begin to add a good regular puppy kibble to the diet and replace the milk mixture with plain baby requirements is a costly mistake. Baby foods are comparatively expensive and do not have the difference in growth between the human infant and the canine infant. A child grows approximately 18 years, a puppy for less than one year (until the skeletal structure is completed).

The dog therefore needs nutritional elements to keep pace with this growth explosion, and these elements are to be found in dog, not human, foods.

You know now how to feed your puppy, so let us find out why he should be fed this way, and go more deeply into foods and supplements and what they can and can't do for your dog's health and growth.

## ESSENTIAL NATURAL FOODS

Your puppy is basically a carnivore, a flesh eater. His teeth are not made for grinding as are human teeth, but are chiefly fashioned for tearing and severing. Over a period of years this fact has led to the erroneous conclusion that the dog must be fed mostly on muscle meat in order to prosper. Wolves, jackals, wild dogs, and foxes comprise the family Canidae to which your dog belongs. These wild relatives of the dog stalk and run down their living food in the same manner the dog would employ if he had not become attached to man. The main prey of these predators are the various hoofed herbivorous animals, small mammals and birds. The carnivores consume the entire body of their prey, not just the muscle meat alone. This manner of feeding has led some zoologists to consider the dog family as omnivorous (eater of both plant and animal matter), despite their obvious physical relationship to the carnivores.

You would assume, and rightly so, that the diet that keeps these wild cousins of the dog strong, healthy and fertile could be depended upon to do the same for your dog. Of course, in this day and age your puppy cannot live off the land. He depends upon you for sustenance, and to feed him properly you must understand what essential food values the wild carnivore derives from his kill, for this is nature's supreme lesson in nutrition.

Babies and puppies may have a lot in common, but not their diets. Feed your new charge a good puppy meal or kibble, not baby food. After all, you wouldn't give puppy chow to a baby, so why would you give a puppy baby food?

The canine hunter first laps the blood of his victim, then tears open the stomach and eats its contents, composed of partly digested vegetable matter. He feasts on the liver, heart, kidneys, lungs and the encrusted intestines. He crushes and consumes the bones and the marrow they

Feedin' time! Your new puppy should be fed at the same times every day to establish a regular routine of eating and elimination.

contain, feeds on fatty meat and connective tissue and finally eats the lean muscle meat. From the blood, bones, marrow, internal organs and muscle meat he has absorbed minerals and proteins. The stomach and its contents have supplied vitamins and carbohydrates. Other proteins come from the ligaments and connective tissue. Hair and some indigestible parts of the intestinal contents provide enough roughage for proper laxation. From the sun he basks in and the water he drinks, he absorbs supplementary vitamins and minerals. From his kill, therefore, the carnivore acquires a well-rounded diet. To supply these same essentials to your dog in a form which you can easily purchase is the answer to his dietary needs.

## DOG FOOD

There are almost as many right diets as there are dog experts, but the basic diet most often recommended is one that consists of a dry food, either meal or kibble form. There are several of excellent quality, manufactured by reliable companies, research tested and nationally advertised. They are inexpensive, highly satisfactory and easily available in stores everywhere in containers of 5 to 50 pounds. Larger amounts cost less per pound, usually.

If you have a choice of brands, it is usually safer to choose the better known one; but even so, carefully read the analysis on the package. Do not choose any food in which the protein level is less than 25 percent, and be sure that this protein comes from both animal and vegetable sources. The good dog foods have meat meal, fish meal, liver and such, plus protein from alfalfa

The most basic and economical diet consists of dry food, in either meal or kibble form. Choose from well-known, established pet shop brands as they generally have spent time and money on research and testing to produce a reliable, high-quality product. Do not choose any food in which the protein level is less than 25 percent.

and soybeans, as well as some dried-milk product. Note the vitamin content carefully. See that they are all there in good proportions; and be especially certain that the food contains properly high levels of vitamins A and D, two of the most perishable and important ones. Note the B-complex level, but don't worry about carbohydrate and mineral levels. These substances are plentiful and cheap and not likely to be lacking in a good brand.

The advice given for how to choose a dry food also applies to moist or canned types of dog foods, if you decide to feed one of these.

Having chosen a really good food, feed it to your dog as the manufacturer directs. And once you've started, stick to it. Never change if you can possibly help it. A switch from one meal or kibble-type food can usually be made without too much upset; however, a change will almost invariably give you (and the dog) some trouble.

**WHEN SUPPLEMENTS ARE NEEDED**

Now what about supplements of various kinds, mineral and

vitamin, or the various oils? They are all okay to add to your dog's food. However, if you are feeding your dog a correct diet, and this is easy to do, no supplements are necessary unless your dog has been improperly fed, has been sick or is having puppies. Vitamins and minerals are naturally present in all the foods; and to ensure against any loss through processing, they are added in concentrated form to the dog food you use. Except on the advice of your

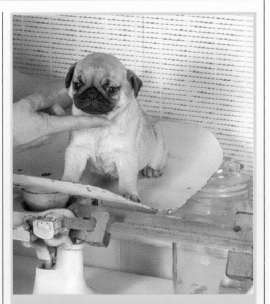

Monitor and record your puppy's weight as he grows—your veterinarian will appreciate your faithful record-keeping.

Vitamin/mineral and other food supplements can be formulated for general nutritional enhancement or to serve particular purposes, such as skin and coat enhancement and /or flea and tick elimination. Photo courtesy of Four Paws.

veterinarian, extra and added amounts of vitamins can prove harmful to your dog! The same risk goes with minerals.

**WATER**

Fresh, cool water should always be available to your dog. This is important to good health throughout his lifetime.

*Water* is one of the elementary nutritional essentials. Considering the fact that the dog's body is approximately 70% water, which is distributed in varying percentages throughout the body tissues and organs, including the teeth and bones, it isn't difficult to realize the importance of this staple to the pup's well being. Water flushes the system, stimulates gastric juice activity, brings about better appetite and acts as a

Water is an essential part of your puppy's diet. Since water is so inexpensive and so important, supply it freely.

Providing fresh, cool water is particularly important when your puppy has been exercising outdoors in hot weather. It is not wise to allow a dog to gulp water in large quantities.

solvent within the body. It is one of the major sources of necessary minerals and helps during hot weather, and to a lesser degree during winter, to regulate the dog's temperature. When a dog is kept from water for any appreciable length of time, dehydration occurs. This is a serious condition, a fact that is known to any dog owner whose animal has been affected by diarrhea, continuous nausea, or any of the diseases in which this form of body shrinkage occurs.

Water is the cheapest part of your dog's diet, so supply it freely, particularly in warm weather. Being so easily provided, so inexpensive and so highly essential to your dog's health, sober thought dictates that we should allow our dogs to "take to drink."

## CALORIC REQUIREMENTS

Caloric requirements vary with age, temperament, changes in temperature and activity. If your pup is nervous, very active, and kept out of doors in winter, his caloric intake must be greater than the phlegmatic, underactive, fully grown dog who has his bed in the house. Keep your puppy in good flesh, neither too fat nor too thin. You are the best judge of the amount to feed him to keep him in his best condition. A well-fed dog should always be clear eyed, glossy-coated, filled with vim and vigor and with enough of an all-over layer of fat to give him sleekness without plumpness.

**The essence of successful training is trust and the complete control of your dog.**

# TRAINING YOUR PUPPY

With sad eyes, a ten-pound puppy can make a sentimental idiot of a tough, two-hundred-pound stevedore. Remember this fact about the wily little rascal when you begin his training. During this early training period a very important factor will be established that will fashion the relationship between you and your dog for the rest of his life. This factor can best be put in the form of a question, a question only you will be able to answer. Who will be the boss, you or your dog?

### CONTROL

The training of your puppy actually began from the moment you brought him home and groomed and housebroke him. During that period you were exerting your will over him and his actions. You were gaining control, and this control is the essence of successful training. The control you have over your puppy will be

The purpose of puppy training is to mold a mannerly dog whose exemplary conduct and obedience make him a pleasure to own and a joy to have with you.

mirrored in the conduct of the grown dog. The purpose of training is to mold a gentlemanly animal whose exemplary conduct and obedience makes him a pleasure to own and a joy to have with you. Like a child, he must be taught manners during the formative period of his life so that a pattern of obedience and good manners is established early. Unlike a child, the formative period is short and so he must be taught quickly and well if he is to mature into an animal of which you can be justly proud. Immediate response to your commands can also be insurance for the dog himself, perhaps saving him some day from a speeding car or some other danger.

The secret of complete control is firmness. Always, when training the puppy, be firm, and insist that he obey once he knows what it is

**This innocent little St. Bernard puppy will one day grow into a 200-pound mammoth. The ability to control such an enormous dog is tantamount to everyone's safety (including the dog's). Training must begin during puppyhood.**

you want of him. Never allow him to perform an act contrary to your wishes.

Other important elements of training are to keep training periods short, lengthen the training time as the pup grows older, use sharp, short and easily understood words of command, approach the training period seriously and have a definite time for it when there will be no outside interruptions, censure your pup when he doesn't obey and praise him or give him a tidbit when he does obey promptly.

**THE TOOLS OF TRAINING**

The equipment necessary to train your pup is simple, unless you later become enamored with obedience work and go on to advanced training. All you need at the beginning for formal training is a choke chain collar, which works on the principle of the noose, and a long leash.

The only other things you need are

determination and the ability to use your voice to convey your wants to the dog. During the housebreaking period you have probably already taught your puppy the meaning of "No," and "Good boy" or "Good girl" so the puppy has probably become familiar with the vocal tone conveying censure and that which means praise. You are now off to a good start!

## COLLAR AND LEASH TRAINING

Most puppies, when purchased just after weaning, have never worn a collar or known the feeling of a leash. Buy a narrow, flat leather collar and allow the puppy to wear it constantly. After he has worn it for a day or two attach a short piece of heavy cord to the collar just about long enough to reach the ground. After dragging this cord around attached to his collar and tripping on it a time or two, the puppy will be partially leash broken, at least to the extent that, when you remove the cord and snap on the leash and gently lead him about, he will not fight the leash.

To make him follow you when on the leash, use short, gentle jerks in the direction toward that you want him to move, rather than a prolonged

Purchase a narrow, flat collar that fits your puppy comfortably. Allow the puppy to wear a collar constantly in preparation for leash training.

pull. Call the puppy's name to get his attention and then add the word, "Come," repeating the single command constantly until the puppy obeys. Never vary the command you use for any specific action. To do so will only confuse the puppy.

When the pup trots along freely on your left side and on a loose leash, tell him he is a "Good boy," indicating how pleased you are that he is such a bright and obedient tyke. A pat and the pleasure in your voice is enough reward. I am not an advocate of the tidbit reward in most instances. Dogs obey their masters because they want to please them and any reward you give is, to the animal, an indication of your pleasure. Making you happy also brings joy to him.

Be content with merely having the pup move freely on leash with only occasionally tangling it around your legs. Rest on your laurels and don't attempt to make the pup rigidly "Heel" until he is four or five months old.

Use short, gentle jerks on the leash when you want your puppy to follow you. With patience and understanding, your puppy will eventually stop fighting and begin following you.

## TRAINING OBSERVATIONS

All that you read in this chapter in reference to training is basic, specifically aimed at training the young puppy; a sort of kindergarten course. Therefore the "Sit" and "Down" commands can be taught while the pup is off leash. Teaching the very young puppy the few necessary basic commands should not be done with the grim, rigid, business-like air employed later in serious training.

Before we go into the "sit" training it might be well to list a few "don'ts" that, if not known, can make training difficult and might even spoil your pup for further training. *Don't* use the leash or your hand as a vehicle of punishment. He will become shy and distrustful of both, shy of the human hand and distrustful of the leash from then on. *Don't* begin teaching the pup a new lesson until the last one has been fully learned. A young canine, like a young human, can only retain a limited amount of teaching at a time. *Don't* constantly shout commands at the puppy. This will only tend to confuse him and he may in time come to think of a command as a reprimand.

## SIT

There are two ways to train a puppy to sit and both ways can be combined successfully in this instance. One is through the active approach and the other is the passive approach. Employing the active approach, you bring the puppy to your left side and, while he is standing on all four feet, you hold your right hand under his chin to

There are two methods to train a puppy to sit: active and passive. This Golden Retriever puppy is being taught to sit using an active, hands-on approach.

prop his forequarters up and gently but firmly press down on his rump, your hand just above where his tail joins the body, until his hindquarters sink to the sit position from pressure. During the process keep quietly repeating the command, "Sit." It is always good practice to preface every command with the dog's name, such as, "Prince, Sit."

When you have accomplished your objective, and the puppy is in the sit position, praise him quietly but lavishly. Keep repeating the command, using voice and hands in the same manner each time. Do about six repetitions. By that time, the pup will have become restless and want to play and further training effort on your part will be wasted.

Repeat the same active training process several times a day and soon the puppy will associate the command with the required action and know exactly what is wanted of him.

Utilizing the passive approach requires constant surveillance. Each time the puppy goes to sit of his own accord you quietly utter the word "Sit." Soon the puppy associates the word-sound and the action that he is doing naturally, is conditioned to respond to the combination of sound and action and will automatically sit when the command is given.

A combination of the two methods, active and passive, generally produces quick results.

## TRAINING TO DOWN

Both active and passive approaches can also be utilized to teach the pup to lie down upon command.

To teach the "Lie Down," or "Down," first give the command to "sit." When the pup has obeyed, push down on the top of his shoulders, until he is forced to lower his forequarters and assume the down position. The given command,

Jumping up on people in greeting is a very annoying habit for your puppy to acquire. Establish a disciplined routine to discourage this behavior.

combined with the required action, is "Prince, Down."

You will find that the down is not as easy to teach as the "Sit." If the puppy is one of the giant breeds, and he resists your downward push to the extent where it becomes almost impossible to accomplish your objective, grasp his front legs above the feet while he is in the sit position, and pull his feet forward to achieve the necessary results.

As mentioned previously the passive approach can be utilized by watching the pup and waiting until he is about to "Down" of his own volition, then voicing the "Down" command as he does. As in the "Sit" training, both approaches can be fruitfully combined.

## SPECIAL TRAINING HINTS

Puppies should always be confined to a specific area when they are left alone, and this area should be chosen for its bareness and lack of adornment that can get a puppy into trouble. Hanging curtains, tapestry, wooden legs on furniture, shoes, socks and many other household articles are all prey to your puppy's playfulness.

Puppies are very curious about their new surroundings and will check out everything they can get their nose in. Therefore, to prevent any unwanted damage to your belongings, or injury to your pup, never leave the puppy alone to roam freely about the house.

Usually, as the pup grows and is given more freedom in the house, he is taught what not to touch but there are a few things most young dogs do that are particularly exasperating and difficult to control. One is stealing food from the table and the other is jumping up on furniture. We can also add jumping up on you and other people in greeting. The latter is particularly annoying if the puppy has been running through mud, and you (or your visitor) are well dressed.

If the pup persists in any or all of these acts, and can't be broken by the usual scolding method, a sure way to get results is through the passive approach. The trick is to have the puppy punish himself and in the process make the result of his disobedience mark itself in his mind so that he won't forget.

Stealing food from the table is an act most puppies can't resist. Their growth pushing them, they are almost constantly hungry and

human food on the table is a delicacy they can't fight. Most puppies who have been scolded harshly for stealing are smart enough not to attempt their crime until you are out of the room. Then they will quietly sneak up to the table and delicately reach for and gobble down any food within reach, especially meat. The way to break them of this habit is to tie a piece of string to a nice piece of meat and set the meat at the edge of the table. To the other end of the string attach a few tin cans, a bell if you have one and anything else that will make a racket. When you are out of the room and the puppy stealthily approaches the table and grabs the meat, he will pull the assortment of noise-makers attached to the other end of the string down from the table. The shock this will cause him would be about the same as a thief would feel who is silently entering a home to steal and, upon opening a window or door, hears an alarm loud enough to

**If jumping up on furniture is undesirable, it should not be tolerated and the puppy should be scolded while in the act.**

**If your puppy persists in jumping up and sleeping on your sofa when you are not around, more drastic measures must be taken. The mousetrap and packaging paper method works very effectively and does no harm to your puppy.**

wake the dead. This is generally a sure cure for puppy's table snatching.

The same kind of approach is used for the pup who persists, even in the face of punishment, upon jumping up and sleeping on the sofa. After repeated punishment he will generally only do this when you are out of the room or the house and jump down as soon as he hears you coming back. Telltale hair on the sofa is the clue to his disobedience. To break a sly tyke of this habit take several mousetraps, set them and put them on the sofa, then gently cover the mousetraps and sofa seats with heavy, large sheets of brown packaging paper. If you are out of the room and you hear the snapping of mousetraps and the yelp of your puppy, you know that you have accomplished your objective. The pup can't be hurt, only startled by the snapping and movement that accompanies it under the paper.

To break your puppy of jumping up on people, grab his forepaws every time he jumps up on you and hold onto them. Do not scold him, instead speak kindly to him, but keep on holding his paws. The position for the puppy will soon become strained and he will try to pull his paws away so he can drop down to all fours. But you must hold onto the front paws until he has become decidedly uncomfortable and is fighting to pull away. He will soon realize that when he jumps up on people he becomes uncomfortable and will quit this action.

### ADVANCED TRAINING

If, in the first four to six months you have housebroken your puppy, taught him to behave on lead, to sit and lie down, not to steal food, not to jump on the sofa or up on people, you have now gone as far as you can in training. After six months more intensive and varied training can begin. If you are interested in going further than merely basic obedience, you cannot begin until your dog is beyond the boisterous playfulness that accompanies puppyhood.

Since this book is written specifically for the neophyte with a first puppy, we will not concern ourselves with the training given the more mature dog. There are many good books on that subject, and almost all populated areas have classes held once a week by competent dog trainers. A telephone call to the secretary of any local dog club, your local veterinarian or dog license bureau will bring you all the necessary information for enrolling yourself and your dog in these training classes.

**Proper obedience training is a responsibility you owe to your puppy. You will find the time spent training your puppy to be a worthwhile, emotionally-fulfilling experience.**

Both the written page and class training should be used to give the puppy a well rounded and advanced education. The personal touch evident in actual class training where you train your dog yourself under the guidance of an experienced dog trainer is important, and being close to other owners with their dogs in obedience classes will help your dog to work closely with you. Here he will learn to obey commands quickly under any circumstances.

Training your dog is as important as training your children. Make your dog a good housedog and pleasant companion through training. Control, patience and common sense combined with proven training procedures is the road to sure success.

# SUGGESTED READING

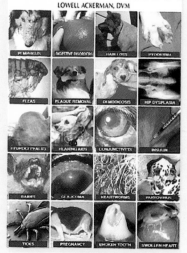

TS-214

TS-204

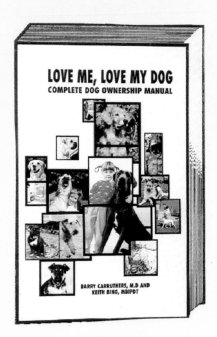

TS-212

TS-205